Scrum You

Your Waterfall Organization Transformed into Multidisciplinary Teams

10 essays on using online tools to improve an offline technique

SCRUM YOUR JIRA!
Your Waterfall Organization Transformed into Multidisciplinary Teams

10 essays on using online tools to improve an offline technique

Published by Clemens Lode Verlag e.K., Düsseldorf

For more information about permission to reproduce selections
from this book, write to contact@lode.de.

2019, Second Edition

ISBN 978-3-945586-70-9

Edited by: *Conna Craig*
Cover design: *Jessica Keatting Graphic Design*
Image sources: *Shutterstock, iStockphoto, pexels.com*
Icons made by http://www.freepik.com from
http://www.flaticon.com is licensed by CC 3.0 BY
(http://creativecommons.org/licenses/by/3.0/)

Printed on acid-free, unbleached paper.
Subscribe to our newsletter. Simply write to newsletter@lode.de or
visit our website.

MANAGEMENT
PSYCHOLOGY

Introduction

神の一手―*Kami no Itte*―Japanese, roughly meaning "move of God" or "godly move"―describes an entirely new insight concerning a move during the game called "Go." Such a move is a goal taught to students to be more attentive toward less obvious maneuvers, leading the students to focus on alternatives. Likewise in management, first put aside the conspicuous answers (like adding more people to an already late project) to make way for an objective mind and attention to alternatives. In management, the challenge is to discover the potential of the team and your organization and to build upon that.

THIS BOOK SHOWS some of the 神の一手―*Kami no Itte*―of management, focused on the Scrum method and the software tool Jira. *Scrum Your Jira* reminds the Scrum Master about the original idea of Agile principles. It teaches how she can implement those in practice, carry on the Agile idea, and become an example for others.

Contents

Publisher's Note

Thank you for keeping up the tradition of reading books. You and your fellow readers have created a market for this book. I hope that I can meet your expectations and I am looking forward to feedback from your side, no matter whether it is positive or negative. To send general feedback, mention the book title in the subject of your message and simply send it to feedback@lode.de. You can also contact us at https://www.lode.de/contact if you are having a problem with any aspect of the book, and we will do our best to address it. Also, we cordially invite you to join our network at https://www.lode.de.

Although I have taken every care to ensure the accuracy of the content, mistakes do happen. If you find an error in one of my books, I would be grateful if you would report this to me. By doing so, you can help me to improve subsequent versions of this book and maybe save future readers from frustration. If you find any errata, please report them by visiting https://www.lode.de/errata, selecting the book title, and entering the details. Once verified, the errata will be uploaded to our website. You will, of course, be credited if you wish.

Best regards,

Clemens Lode
CEO, Lode Publishing
Düsseldorf, Germany, September 1st, 2019

Preface

 Nurture your mind with great thoughts; to believe
in the heroic makes heroes.

—Benjamin Disraeli

Tthe decision to write this book began with an insight that Scrum is much more than a set of meetings and boards. But then again, that *is* the idea of what Scrum is: lean project management, without all the documents. It is also a buzzword, with companies wanting to copy the success of other organizations that have fully (and successfully) implemented Agile principles.

I guess I have to admit that to truly understand something, I need to "build" it one way or another. Despite the subject of my previous book, *Philosophy for Heroes: Knowledge*, inter-personal and management ideas come more naturally to me than abstract philosophical principles. So, instead of writing down everything I have learned about Scrum over the course of several years, I wrote these articles over the course of one week each—in a truly Agile way (followed by some editing to give it a coherent message). It is up to you to decide if this experiment was a success!

This book is about Scrum and Jira, the most popular management technique and the most popular ticketing system. It is written in a light-hearted tone, similar to how you might chat with a fellow consultant about your experiences implementing Scrum or Jira. The main message is that there is more to Scrum and Jira than meet the eye because Scrum is more than a series of meetings.

My hope is that you will take with you one or two interesting thoughts from this book, and develop them further. Personally, I would like to place this book in the hands of a younger version of myself, someone who finds himself at the beginning of his professional career, ready to start new projects. Even if I reach only a small handful of people who will take to heart a few of these core ideas and set out to lead projects better, I will be able to enjoy the rewards of this book.

Do you need help with the Agile process in your company? Subscribe to our newsletter at https://www.lode.de/agile or contact us for coaching at coach@lode.de.

Best regards,

Clemens Lode
Author, *Scrum Your Jira!*
Düsseldorf, Germany, August 1st, 2019

An Introduction... to Rugby

> We scrum for possession, run for the try zone, bleed for the team, and live for the game.

The origin of Scrum is in sports, namely rugby. Unfortunately, connecting the name ("Scrum") to the sport is usually where knowledge about the roots of Scrum ends. But I think it is worthwhile to take a look at how teams win games in sports. Other than the name, you will discover many similarities between the development process and Scrum. Also, as a Scrum Master, becoming aware of this background will provide you with a great analogy to explain the Scrum rituals to your team.

Basically, rugby is similar to European soccer and American football: two teams trying to get the ball to the other side. Figure 1 shows several differences that make each of the three games unique in their playing style:

	Rugby	**Football**	**Soccer**
Goal:	touchdown	touchdown	goal
Pass forward:	no	partial	mostly
Block:	ball owner	anyone	passive
Moves:	continuous	interruptions	continuous

Figure 1: Comparison of different sport games

While there a number of other differences (protection, penalties, etc.), the properties listed in the table lead to significantly different playing styles for each game.

- In **rugby**, with the objective of having to be near the goal (touchdown), there is little danger from scoring a lucky win from afar. Also, no forward passing is allowed; the team has to actually run together to the other side, creating the need for a cohesive team with quickly changing roles.

- **Soccer** mitigates that by having a separate goalkeeper role. In terms of field movement, soccer motivates the team to spread out. Fast-moving forward passes, together with the lack of the ability to physically block the other teams' players, are the main causes for this.

- In **football**, forward passes are allowed, but so is blocking—making the field of operation much smaller. Football is slower than rugby or soccer, given regular interruptions between moves. This way, it becomes more strategic. Also, this gives room for a lot more communication between the players and the coach. The team might have to be less independent than in rugby or soccer.

This comparison gives you several hints about why rugby, and not soccer or football, was used as the blueprint for Scrum. It goes far beyond giving it a cool name. In Scrum, while you have your specialists, they are all on the field. There is less communication with management (coaches in football), and the product owner is part of the team. The rugby team does not have fixed specialized roles, like a goalkeeper or a quarterback. Depending on your software team's cultural background, teach them the differences between football in the US and soccer in Europe. Watch a few rugby matches together (team building!) and discuss how this applies to the situation in your company. It is an excellent way of opening people up. By seeing it "in action," your team can more easily understand the abstract and product development-related terms and concepts. In fact, I encourage you to watch a few minutes of rugby right now to get into the mood.

Back? OK! Now imagine the rugby players using Jira instead of co-ordinating everything on the field. An impossibility! That is where this book comes in, tackling the problems related to using Scrum with Jira, and opening your eyes about how to examine the use of Jira in your organization.

Now get ready for the kick-off!

Chapter 1

Implementing Agile Techniques

 Our Scrum Is Special!

> The Agile movement provides alternatives to traditional project management. Agile approaches help teams respond to unpredictability with incremental, iterative work cadences and empirical feedback. Agilists propose alternatives to Waterfall, or traditional sequential development.

—The Agile Movement (edited)[1]

> Scrum is an Agile software development model based on multiple small teams working in an intensive and interdependent manner. The term is named for the scrum (or scrummage) formation in rugby, which is used to restart the game after an event that causes play to stop, such as an infringement.

—What is Scrum?[2]

When clients ask me to help with implementation of Agile techniques by using Scrum, my first question is: "What do you mean by 'Scrum'?" Usually, I then hear that the company has its own special version of Scrum (or other Agile technique) because, according to the people with whom I am meeting, their company is a special case.

First, yes, your company is a special case. Each company is unique and in a particular market niche. Second, if you followed the evolutionary approach of improvements in small increments, you have adapted your process to the environment of the company. No two companies are alike. Hence your need for an external consultant to examine the conditions in your company.

---

[1] AgileMethodology, 2008.
[2] TechTarget, 2007.

The reality I see all too often is that a company hires a Scrum Master who merely acts as a supporting firefighter, accompanying the former project manager (now "product owner") and running around the company putting out fires. This kind of extra resource is justified to upper management by pointing to "Agile" and its use in other companies...

Introducing (and running) Scrum means that you want to change your company according to proven methods. You cannot have your cake (Scrum) and eat it, too (changing Scrum to suit your company) —you cannot improve your company by adapting the Scrum process to your company. Obviously, you cannot change your whole company in one day—it might take years! But the *goal* should be clear: to take all the steps necessary to become truly Agile instead of finding rationalizations about why your company is a special case.

Waterfall · *Waterfall* is a project management method where a product moves through several phases before a final version is finished for release. Compared to Agile, the problem with this method is that it requires additional communication channels between phases. Also, the time until a team or company gets feedback from a customer is generally much longer.

Scrum · *Scrum* is a set of management tools that focuses a project back on the team level and uncovers internal and external impediments of the production process. By reducing communication paths through small, multidisciplinary teams, as well as frequent releases to the customer for review, the probability for project success can be improved even if the scope is not clear from the start. In addition, work is divided into units of fixed lengths (sprints), which helps to plan future sprints with your team working at a sustainable speed.

Sprint · A *sprint* is a timespan of one to four weeks within which a selection of stories should be finished by the team. Given the fact that the whole team spends 10 percent of the time (depending on the sprint length) planning and reviewing each sprint, the goal is to reach 100 percent completion of all stories while meeting the project's quality standards and without overtime. Like a marathon runner needs to carefully plan her energy, planning a sprint requires excellent estimation skills by the teams.

SCRUM MASTER · The *Scrum Master* controls the Scrum process. Besides proactively identifying and removing impediments to the process, the Scrum Master also supports the team in meetings as a moderator and individually in personal talks. The Scrum Master also stands up against outside influence on the process, ideally by propagating the Agile idea throughout the organizations and by explaining why certain restrictions are necessary for the overall project success.

PRODUCT OWNER · The *product owner* is part of the Scrum team and represents the stakeholders. The main task is stakeholder management as well as having a deep understanding of what the project is about and being able to make decisions. A product owner fills and prioritizes the backlog, keeping the complexity estimations of the team in mind. The product owner should have full authority and the final say about the prioritization of the backlog. During the sprint, the product owner answers questions from the team about the scope of the project, as well as gives feedback about finished (but not necessarily done!) tasks, but otherwise does not interfere in how the team manages its work.

Looking at the actual causes of problems

One of the techniques used in project management is to find the cause of an issue. Digging deeper, my next set of questions to the client usually focuses on the greater picture or vision of the company. Instead of telling me about their mission, they typically respond that they want to "test" Agile and then implement it in other parts of the company. Besides noting the misunderstanding of Agile as the new (local!) management technique, questions arise: What would success look like? What would failure look like? What are the concrete, measurable business objectives of the project of introducing Agile?

I am convinced that introducing Agile itself should be managed with modern project management techniques, PMBOK being my favorite. Managing Agile goes far beyond the scope of this chapter, but you certainly must have an idea about where you are going with it and what you want to achieve.

> **PMBOK®** · *PMBOK* stands for *Project Management Body of Knowledge* and describes a generic system of workflows within a project. While it is mainly applied to Waterfall projects, many of its parts can also be used in an Agile project, like defining how the team communicates with the outside world, defining the vision and scope of the project, or defining why one would want to use Scrum at all. (PMI, 2013)

To illustrate this further, I recommend reading Ayn Rand's introduction to philosophy that looks at the example of an astronaut stranded on a planet:

> Suppose that you are an astronaut whose spaceship loses control and crashes on an unknown planet. When you regain consciousness and find that you are not badly hurt, the first three questions on your mind would be: Where am I? How can I find out? What should I do?
>
> You see unfamiliar vegetation outside, and there is air to breathe; the sunlight seems paler than you remember it and colder. You turn to look at the sky, but stop. You are struck by a sudden feeling: if you don't look, you won't have to know that you are, perhaps, too far from Earth and no return is possible. So long as you don't know it, you are free to believe what you wish—and you experience a foggy, pleas-

ant, but somehow guilty, kind of hope.

You turn to your instruments: they may be damaged, you don't know how seriously. But you stop, struck by a sudden fear: how can you trust these instruments? How can you be sure that they won't mislead you? How can you know whether they will work in a different world? You turn away from the instruments.

Now you begin to wonder why you have no desire to do anything. It seems so much safer just to wait for something to turn up somehow; it is better, you tell yourself, not to rock the spaceship. Far in the distance, you see some sort of living creatures approaching; you don't know whether they are human, but they walk on two feet. They, you decide, will tell you what to do.

You are never heard from again.

This is fantasy, you say? You would not act like that and no astronaut ever would? Perhaps not. But this is the way most men live their lives, here, on Earth.

—Ayn Rand, *Address to the Graduating Class of the United States Military Academy at West Point New York* (adapted)[3]

In terms of a company, your immediate goal is of course to survive the next month. But then, you have to establish where you are on the map. You have to open your eyes, look at the sky, and check your instruments.

In terms of Agile, I recommend to my clients that they run it like a project. We know what works from hundreds of studies, and we can create a list of items that are implemented in Scrum. In that list, we simply mark the current state of the process. Often, even in non-Agile companies, some processes have already been implemented because the people who are managing projects notice which processes

---

[3]Rand, 1974.

work. A simple approach is to check again the *Principles Behind the Agile Manifesto*[4]:

- Welcome changing requirements.

- Trust and motivate individuals on your team and other teams in the company.

- Developers and non-developers (e.g., marketers, salespeople) must work together daily.

- Face-to-face is the most efficient and effective method of getting things done.

- Progress is measured in terms of working software.

- The entire team must promote sustainable development, they should be able to maintain a constant pace indefinitely.

- The entire team must work together to continuously improve technical excellence and to enhance agility.

- Keep in mind that simplicity is valuable; simplicity is the art of maximizing the amount of work not done.

- The best solutions emerge from self-organizing teams.

- Effective teams regularly reflect on how to become more effective.

- An Agile company satisfies customers through early, frequent, and continuous delivery.

Together with the client, for each point, I detail how this is implemented in the company—this is the first step of documenting the current process. If I am not able explain how it is implemented or if we find that it is not implemented at all, I focus on those points and try to find explanations for each: why the company is not able or not willing to fulfill this part of the Agile process. And I do not just ask, "Why?" I ask, "Why why why why why...?" until I find

---

[4]Beck, 2001.

out the actual reasons something has not been implemented.[5] *And at this point, the real work starts: addressing those issues that hinder the Agile process on a daily basis.*

---

[5] Ohno, 2006.

Chapter 2

Multidisciplinary Teams in Scrum

- The most efficient and effective method of conveying information to and within a development team is face-to-face conversation.

- Business people and developers must work together daily throughout the project.

- Build projects around motivated individuals. Give them the environment and support they need, and trust them to get the job done.

- The best architectures, requirements, and designs emerge from self-organizing teams.

—Principles Behind the Agile Manifesto[1]

Working in multidisciplinary teams is one of the main success criteria in Scrum. It is crucial to have different elements of the project —including the user or customer—represented on one team. In reality, in my work with clients, I often see that their move to Agile consisted only of changing the management style of a team, and in most cases, this applied only to the software developer team. It is no surprise, then, that I often hear a description of the situation that goes something like this: "OK, we have this software development team here, and we want to test out Scrum. Now, we are looking for a Scrum Master. Oh, yes, and we have worked with Scrum for several years, but it is not working. Maybe you can help?"

My initial questions to a client revolve around what is not working and whether Scrum was set up as a project (see Chapter 1). I then focus on one of the points listed in the Agile Manifesto, namely multidisciplinary teams. What is a multidisciplinary team? Does creating such a team mean that you have to mix Java and Android program-

---

[1]Beck, 2001.

mers? Or that people on the team should have some PHP experience if a website is involved somewhere in the project?

Actually, multidisciplinary teams are one of the core principles of Agile, as opposed to Waterfall. To understand the benefits of multidisciplinary teams, let us first take a closer look at what the Waterfall method (which does not incorporate this approach) looks like.

The first essential step in setting up a company is assembling the right group of employees. In a company following the Waterfall method, ads for jobs are written for and specialists are hired to do specific tasks, like programming, marketing, sales, or editing. Each person works in his or her specialized field with maximum efficiency.

Initially, the specialists form a common team, a handful of people working together on one project. With the growth of the company, new people are hired, and each specialist will lead individual teams; the former specialists become managers, and each team gets its own room, its own planning, its own resource allocation, etc.

Depending on the environment (startup vs. large, existing company), the course of a company can vary widely, but essentially, in companies that have not adopted Agile, you will usually find specialized departments each performing a task with maximum efficiency. Sounds great, right? You have the best people working in specialized departments highly attuned to their tasks. What could go wrong?

What could go wrong is that this kind of departmentalization will most likely lead to the use of the Waterfall management method—at any given time, a department works on one phase of the product. First, it goes through design, then development, editing, quality assurance, marketing, and finally publishing and sales, with the managers busy with tons of meetings, cross-department communication, and resource balancing. With multiple teams, it is nearly impossible to have one team ready to start the next phase just as another team finishes. Ultimately, this leads to long release cycles —sometimes years-long.

Then, people hear about Scrum. And what do they do? They take individual teams, set up a product owner and Scrum Master for each team, set up a ticketing system, sprints, and more meetings—with the managers still busy communicating and negotiating resources between the teams. The result? Marginal effects, somewhat more disciplined development teams (mostly because of more investment into the build systems to allow more frequent releases), and a story to tell all the developers that now, with Scrum, everything will be better and will continue to improve over time.

I hate to break it to you, but this is Scrum in name only. Specialized teams cannot deliver anything but concepts or work packages. Suddenly, the users are no longer the customers—instead, the "customers" become the next team. Eventually, only one department (sales) ever faces an actual customer who will use the product.

Now, moving from the phase-based management of Waterfall to Agile, *how can companies benefit from having multidisciplinary teams?*

Break with the idea of departments and focus on products (or features). Put together all the people—including marketing, design, and sales—who will deliver the final project. Does that mean that the salespeople have to learn Java and the tech guys have to do sales? Well, yes, to some extent. At least they have to learn how to deliver a product together and help each other out. Ideally, this would have begun during the hiring process, recruiting people who are good in one area, and also know a little bit about all the other aspects of product development. If you have only specialists, have them work in pairs (two people, one computer) on features, allowing easy knowledge transfer between departments. Also, even in early development, there is a lot to do for everyone. The salesperson might not develop a new API, but he or she can help with testing, meeting with clients, preparing presentations, advocating the team's ideas within the company, creating beta- and sales channels, setting up newsletters and landing pages—all tasks marketing and sales could start doing early on, in addition to learning how the product works from the inside.

For an established company, this is a long road. But your competitor has already started doing it, and your only advantage is that you (still) have more resources than the startup next door. When will your organization improve and become genuinely Agile?

When it comes to multidisciplinary teams, how is your company doing? How are the teams in your company structured? Does that structure support information exchange between departments or specialization of individuals? How are HR decisions integrated into your Agile strategy?

Chapter 3

Scrum and Jira: A Love-Hate Relationship

Steps to Bring Your Agile Project Back on Track

Within a company, Scrum is usually initiated in software teams, because they are the teams who have to deal with the biggest insecurities in terms of planning. Each software project is an entirely new project, even if it is "just" a new version. The software market changes rapidly, hence Agile methods are the management method of choice.

There is a glitch in the system, though: hiring people based on their computer skills often comes at a price, namely interpersonal communication. The HR department of a company should take great care to not just hire the best individual coders, but instead, people who can communicate effectively and have high emotional intelligence.[1]

> **JIRA** · The on-premise or cloud software *Jira* by Atlassian is one of the leading ticketing systems available. Beyond a mere ToDo list, it provides administration functionality for projects, Scrum and Kanban boards, custom workflows, custom screens, user rights management, plugins, and third-party integration. The name itself stems from Bugzilla, the software Atlassian used initially for bug tracking. They began calling it by the Japanese name for Godzilla, "Gojira." When they later developed their own bug tracker, they just dropped the Go—hence Jira! (see https://confluence.atlassian.com/pages/viewpage.action?pageId=223219957)

We are a culture that loves technology—sometimes to the exclusion of working with people. As a result, our communication tools tend to be complicated and directed at an audience of software engineers. This also applies to Jira, which is often used to manage the Agile process. But is that really a good decision?

The gold standard of Scrum is face-to-face communication. To what extent is your team practicing this? I recommend taking another look at the *Principles Behind the Agile Manifesto*[2], *What Google*

---

[1]Duhigg, 2016.
[2]Beck, 2001.

Learned from its Quest to Build the Perfect Team[3], and Chapter 1 on the subject. Then, as a first step, evaluate where you are in the process of becoming an Agile company. Do you think your Jira installation helps or hinders your progress?

In the previous chapter, I wrote about the importance of multidisciplinary teams. Tools highly optimized for use with software developers might cause problems when other departments are expected to use them, or when creating a team with a mix of people with different specializations. A company has to be careful not to focus on what is most effective for only part of the company but should instead look at the company (or a given product) as a whole. How well a company is doing in that regard is visible by a quick look into its Jira user directory: if you see only developers having logged in recently, the system is more an obstacle than a useful tool for communication between the teams.

I doubt you will ditch Jira just because of this book, though. I rely heavily on Jira. It is likely that you are reading this book because you are already using Jira, and you will probably not dismantle Jira any time soon! So, with the system already in place and the information already managed within Jira, how can we make it visible to the rest of the company?

In that regard, Jira is a step back in terms of Agile, as it disconnects people and makes things overcomplicated. What we need to do is recognize the drawbacks of Jira and examine ways around them.

For example, when creating new stories, Jira gives you the option to write a summary and a description. This immediately leads people to come up with a descriptive name as the "summary," and enter the actual user story "As a user, ..." in the description (if at all).

---

[3]Duhigg, 2016.

My proposal is that the description field should be used only for the *acceptance criteria* and the *definition of done* (see Chapter 4). Descriptions should *not* be needed or even seen by anyone outside the Scrum team. Hence, **put the user story into the summary!** Your backlog board will look much more structured if all the stories follow a similar naming scheme. Nobody outside the team will be in a rush to look at your board if it is filled with technical jargon. And if we take a step back, that is actually what Scrum teaches: Create a board with stickers describing user stories! Why not do exactly that? Having less (e.g., just a sticker) sometimes is better than having 50 customizable fields. Hence, it makes sense to fill a product backlog with tasks to resemble a physical board with stickers.

Another example is epics. These are used differently from company to company; some call it a "bigger story," some call it a "feature," for others it is a "project." If you are using Jira, you first have to focus on defining an "epic," then on how it is displayed. How would you implement epics when using nothing but paper stickers?

In Jira, epics are essentially "super-stories." Why? Because Jira offers you a progress bar for each epic. (As this really reminds me of a pre-planned Waterfall project, I find this feature useless.) Much more interesting is the rather simple feature of color. Assigning epics to stories quickly gives you an idea what the story is about, as each epic shows up as a colored banner on the board. With epics, the Jira board comes alive: you can quickly and easily make visual sense of the entire project—where you are at, what is left to do, and who is going to do it. For example, in the past, I often used "Frontend," "Backend," and "IT" as three main epics when working on a pure server project (in a non-Agile business environment). On the board, you immediately see what type of stories there are. Of course once the Scrum process is fully adopted, you should utilize user-facing features (as opposed to system components) as epics.

Here, I will leave you with a final point. It is a small issue, yet one that annoys the perfectionist in me whenever I start looking at a Jira board of a new client: the "priority" field. In Scrum, there is no "priority" field. First, within a sprint, it is up to the team which tasks to work on and in what order. If you, as a product owner, want to direct the exact sequence of which tasks are built, that is eXtreme Programming (XP), a topic for later. Second, even if you take priority into account, who determines the priority? Certainly not the reporter, who might have no idea about the business value or the time needed to implement it, yet who is prompted, by Jira, to fill out the form (better to leave it empty than fill in a meaningless bit of information that will just cause more work for the one reading it). And the product owner already sorts the backlog according to priority, based on business value and estimation. The usual result is that in the Jira backlog, you end up with two types of priorities—critical and urgent—because every reporter thinks his task is kind of important. The priority even shows up as little red arrows—completely unnecessary and confusing.

> **BACKLOG** · The *backlog* of a project is a list of stories prioritized by the product owner according to the business value of each (estimated by the stakeholders and product owner) and complexity (estimated by the team). Keeping a clean backlog is key to success: it is not an idea graveyard! You can move all those nice-to-have stories to a separate list.

Unfortunately, Jira does not allow you to deactivate priorities directly. There is a little trick, though: In the project settings, in the priority scheme, you can create a new default priority and upload an empty transparent PNG file as the corresponding icon. This solves the problem and the board looks a little more like a real Scrum board!

How does your team use Jira in your Scrum process? What are your remedies to Jira's drawbacks? Do you ever simply leave Jira aside and use a pen and paper?

Chapter 4

Automate Your Definition of Done

Reduce Repetitive Work by Employing a Smart Workflow

Let us first define our concepts. In Scrum practice, we have basically four kinds of tasks the team can work on:

> **ACCEPTANCE CRITERIA** · The *acceptance criteria* are a story-specific set of conditions that need to be met for the story to be accepted and checked off by the product owner. A better expression for acceptance criteria is actually "business-facing tests."

> **DEFINITION OF DONE** · The *definition of done* is a story-independent list of general tasks that apply to all stories to ensure proper quality assurance, documentation, testing, and so on. This list can grow over time.

> **SUBTASKS** · *Subtasks* are specific and usually unique pieces of work related to a particular new feature. If we find that, over the course of many stories, certain types of subtasks repeat, we can elevate them to *definition of done*—like "updated documentation" or "added unit tests."

Implementing *acceptance criteria* and the *definition of done* in Jira is a challenge: there is no defined field for those except for the description field. For tasks with repeating *acceptance criteria*, there is no alternative to adding them to new tasks again and again. Likewise, the *definition of done* is too long to always be copied into tasks and is usually put into a separate document. The drawback of this solution is that it is labor intensive and will ultimately lead to sloppiness:

- items of the *definition of done* get ignored,

- *acceptance criteria* are forgotten,

- the board columns are misused to mark the status of a task in regard to the *acceptance criteria* (testing, documentation, etc.), or even

- separate subtasks are created for each *acceptance criteria.*

What to do? Part of the *definition of done* can be enforced by the continuous integration system. Every commit could be automatically checked for unit tests or code quality in general (e.g., using the tool *Checkstyle*). While I encourage this very strongly, it will not cover everything... what to do with the *acceptance criteria* and *definition of done*? How do we implement these in Jira? Well, there are better, automated solutions—with Jira.

First, some organization is required. Even if we find a way to add the *definition of done* automatically, the list is typically in bad shape and requires additional thinking by the team when implementing stories. For example, maybe it is a story with business value, but it does not need any programming. Think of editing a page in a content management system like WordPress: asking for unit tests might cause some bewildered looks. Hence, we need categories for different groups of *definition of done*. Luckily, with epics, we have already created such categories. We might just have to double-check and cross-reference with our *definition of done*. For example, a publishing company might require that all WordPress articles show a featured image. We have an epic called "WordPress article," and for each story within this epic, we add a *definition of done* element including the check for a featured image.

How do we do that in practice?

Instead of adding subtasks for each *definition of done* item to a story, we add them to the story as *checkboxes*. For this, we need a plugin. There are two options, depending on whether you run your Jira in the cloud (yourjiraname.atlassian.net) or on your own server.

> **ISSUE CHECKLIST FOR JIRA** · The *Issue Checklist for Jira* add-on allows users to add simple ToDo list items to an issue and watch the progress when items from the list are completed. It is only available on the Atlassian Marketplace for a Jira Cloud installation (*Issue Checklist* 2017)—check *Simple Tasklists* 2017 for a similar plugin for a Jira Server installation.

Using the plugin, a developer can easily mark which parts of the *definition of done* are complete, and the product owner can track the progress as well. Also, we can add the *acceptance criteria* to the list. This is all nicely integrated into the workflow with templates! It even makes the description box mostly superfluous; remember that the story itself goes into the summary line!

In case you need more control of the story creation process (like adding special instructions to the description), you need to change the workflow yourself. This is a little bit of hacking as we need to add a separate transition for each type of story. Any global instructions can be added to the initial "Create" transition of your workflow. Those will be added to all new stories. If your instructions differ only from project to project, not from epic to epic, you can create individual transitions for each project. If you use the epic-based approach, mentioned before, you will need to add another state. Let us call it "Ready," meaning that the definition of ready is fulfilled (all the *acceptance criteria* and *definition of done* are entered and the story is formally correct).

> **DEFINITION OF READY** · The *definition of ready* is an agreement between the team and the stakeholders (represented by the product owner) that new stories have to conform to a certain standard

before they are added to a sprint. It is up to the product owner to make sure that the team has sufficient information to know what the individual story is about and when it is accepted (*acceptance criteria, definition of done*). Obviously, the Scrum Master can help to clean up the stories so that they also conform in terms of visual and grammatical formatting.

From the initial "Open" status, create one new transition for each group of epics, with individual "Update Description Field" commands. You can even combine the global instructions from the "Create" transition with the later "Ready" transition. Another option is to directly fill out the epic field by the transition, with a lot of buttons in your initial detail view of the issue.

Whether you use the plugin's features or the manual workflow approach (or both), a big plus of this approach is that you can centrally control the instructions you want to add to stories. All new stories of all your teams will automatically contain the current set of instructions. You will not need to waste lengthy meetings to update every single user of your Jira system to include a proper list, nor will you have to spend endless hours fixing invalid entries.

Chapter 5

In Scrum, Ownership Matters

Moving from "Command and Control" to "Innovative Agile Management"

"Ownership" describes how a knowledge worker needs to be part of the whole process and not just a specialist in a department.

The idea of business as we know it today was created in the early 20th century. Before, each factory worker had a very specific task designed and planned by a manager. With more complex products and specialization, more decisions had to be made during the project by employees instead of beforehand by management. Ultimately, the idea of a "knowledge worker" was created. Problems were no longer solved on the business level, products were no longer clones, every product was individually crafted and new. Workers ceased to be "copying machines" and became inventors, communicators, and researchers. In today's high-tech world, micromanaging a knowledge worker is only possible if you already know the solution and all the steps involved. A low-risk project with predictable outcome is perfect for the Waterfall method. But if you do not know the market or technology, it is up to the team to work out the solution on their own, ideally with an Agile technique.

Scrum recognizes this change by putting the Scrum team at the center of development. In order to produce something relevant for the customer in a quickly changing market, the team needs to feel a sense of ownership, not only in the confines of their specialty or department but also of the overall product. But this is in conflict with the old Waterfall thinking: the Scrum team is seen by management as incapable of making the right business decisions—and often rightfully so because HR hired developers, but not people with business, marketing, or sales experience! Last but not least, upper management actually removes experts from teams to "promote" them to middle management as a "reward."

In reality, the situation is more complicated. Striking the right balance between business and development is difficult. But this difficulty is mostly rooted in the fact that in order to implement these Agile ideas, established systems within the company have to move away from separate departments and the Waterfall method. It comes down to the ultimate question: *Do you really want an Agile team?* Or do you want to keep important decisions outside the team and enforce a system of command and control, moving and managing work packages from team to team?

Now, which parts of Scrum are affected by this? Or, a better question would be: in your existing implementation of Scrum, how do you recognize symptoms relating to a team's lack of feeling of ownership?

I will explain three examples to illustrate:

A demand for commitment and overtime. Directly or indirectly, a manager might interpret the idea that sprints are planned as a contract of delivery with the team. On first glance, Scrum very much seems like an external company contractually bound to deliver a particular set of features in a certain amount of time (a sprint). As a consequence, this leads to a lot of failed sprints, high employee turnover, higher salary demands, or even the installation of the Scrum Master as someone who pressures the team to perform. This led to an update of Scrum in 2011: the word "commitment" was replaced with "forecast." The idea of Scrum is not to be able to create perfect sprints which will, in the end, deliver exactly as promised. If that is required, and if your business depends on such a model of planning, use a different method. If you need the output of Scrum in another department precisely at the "promised" date, you are practicing the Waterfall method, not Scrum! Even in large-scale Scrum, the planning of the new sprint does not start weeks ahead, trying to include the results of other teams. It begins on the first day of your sprint. The right way to deal with dependencies between teams is to restructure them so that they can work independently.

Additional meetings. Beyond your regular Scrum meetings, a lot of other meetings might happen that involve the Scrum Master, product owner, or members of the Scrum team. This is usually taken as something normal. But I suggest carefully logging and looking at each of these meetings. The findings might hold valuable information about the quality of your Scrum process. Ask the questions:

- *Why exactly is this meeting being held?* A meeting with upper management about the course of the product might point to a lack of ownership on the part of the team or poor attendance by upper management in sprint reviews.

- *Who exactly is needed for the meeting in question?* If meetings always include everyone, this might point to a lack of scope and planning. Maybe two or three people are enough to discuss an important technical issue. Perhaps backlog refinement requires only part of the team.

- *What about non-formal meetings that interrupt the work of the team?* Some meetings could be delayed and made part of the regular Scrum meetings.

- *Could this meeting be replaced by an e-mail?* Some meetings can be prevented altogether if one person sits down and prepares the topic in detail. Even if a meeting is then still necessary, you will have a concrete agenda, and the attendees are up to date when it starts. Companies like Amazon go as far as demanding four written pages as preparation for each meeting and reserving half an hour at the beginning of each meeting for the attendees to study it.

Deployment, demo, or installation issues. Encountering issues at the very last "phase" of the project is a common problem, yet it points to a much larger issue, especially if the demo is seen as work that can be squeezed in at the end of the sprint. As with all bugs, you can and should trace these particular issues back to the origin and find out the reason they were made (for example, was the demo made at the end of the sprint during overtime hours?). Given an issue's particular place of occurrence, you should focus on:

- *Project and test planning.* Having bugs in one specific place means that there is an imbalance in the parts of the program you test. In the Waterfall method, the parts developed first underwent more testing and more changes than the later parts. In Agile, your goal should be to have all parts equally tested.

- *Non-involvement of the team in the deployment phase.* Looking back at my history as a programmer, I always felt the need to take extra care when I was the final person responsible for delivery. I did so because I would be the one staying up late at night to fix the issue when customers came complaining. *I felt ownership.*

- *Scrapped projects or features after development.* This happens. Unfortunately, often way too late because no decision could be made within the company, and responsibilities were pushed from one desk to another within the company hierarchy. It is due to a lack of connection between the customer and the Scrum team. It might point to non-involvement of the team in the final phase of the project. And that is not testing or deployment, it is getting the product to the customer! If it is an internal project, it means getting it to upper management. If you see an increase in developed projects or features being scrapped, you are either increasingly falling back to the Waterfall method, or your team does not have marketing or sales expertise.

To summarize: Keep your eyes and ears open. Situations such as a lack of motivation or ownership by the team should not be accepted, but the cause of such issues often lies much deeper, below the surface. As a Scrum Master, you are like a medical doctor, looking for clues about the underlying issues.

Chapter 6

Keep Some Energy in Reserve

What Is the Goal of a Scrum Sprint?

A sprint consists of several stories that the team needs to complete, and each story has a number of points assigned to it. But what is the goal of a sprint? Some stories might not be finished at the end, so is it to produce as many story points as possible? Let us assume that indeed the goal of a Scrum sprint would be to produce as many story points as possible. Force the team to work overtime! OK, that does not work because it is not sustainable. On average, you will end up with decreased productivity as the bugs will pile up and your team will be demotivated or even get sick.

What else can we adjust? We could be optimistic: let's just add as many stories as possible into the sprints. If the team was able to do X story points before, it might be able to do that again! What is the result of this? Even though you might end up (at least, in the beginning) with more finished story points on average in your sprints, consider the following disadvantages:

- You will end up more often than not with unfinished sprints.
- There will be constant pressure on the team to be faster (as opposed to producing more value for the customer—which is not necessarily the same).
- There is no longer a goal.
- If the sprint cannot be completed because of too many tasks, the sprint as a concept loses its meaning and becomes more like a backlog.

Because in Scrum the team decides which tasks to work on and in what order, "uncomfortable" (but maybe valuable) tasks might remain unfinished (there is always something "more important" coming up) and dragged along to future sprints. The product owner then has to require people to conduct work in a specific order, and the concept of a sprint again loses its meaning, and the team loses its sense of responsibility for the sprint.

The point is that you can fool yourself into thinking that an increase of story points per sprint (if that happens at all, considering the first two points in the list above) actually leads to a higher business value. The concept of "more story points equals better" is actually the cause of delay. If you are dragging half-finished stories along, their business value will remain at zero, no matter how much work has been put into them.

Stories that are worked on over the course of many sprints become more expensive, as their business value remains unrealized and people have to remember again and again what they were about. They also slow down planning and impede the focus of the team when selecting the next story to work on.

"Management thinking"—the idea that 100 percent workload of the team will maximize the business value of the project—is faulty. From a management point of view, this idea has a scary outlook: your team completed its work and now... what? Do you send them home? Do you have them start another sprint? Do you add new stories to the completed sprint?

It is essential to get away from the idea of 100 percent workload being optimal. That is local optimization to a more global problem. When the team is done with the sprint, the team is done! Let the team decide what to do with the remaining time. People are self-motivated, they generally like to learn. Give them the opportunity to read books, attend conferences or seminars, research new technologies, or just take a break. Use the time for team-building, improving the office atmosphere, or generally cleaning up things that have piled up (there is always something). Encourage them to discuss what projects or program parts could be scrapped. But let it be the team's time. Set the completion of sprints as the goal and have the team celebrate their success!

If you are afraid that, with such a positive outlook, they will aim for less and less each sprint, re-examine your own views and ask the five "why" questions, beginning with: Why are they not motivated to want to work on the project? Asking that question of yourself is much more productive than trying to coerce your team into working more... which usually just means having them spend more time in the office staring at the screen without really being more productive. Yes, the team has to lead the project; it is theirs. If you are not comfortable with that idea, maybe Agile methods are not for you. But if you are, team ownership of the product is essential.

As a side note, if you really want to maximize the story points, maybe eXtreme Programming (XP) is for you (this is another Agile method). Here, there are no "sprints" but the team works together on one task at a time—with the product owner determining the sequence of the tasks. The advantage is that individual tasks are finished as quickly as possible, with the whole team behind them. You get quick returns, although at the cost of not being able to utilize parallel work, plus the possible overhead—just imagine seven people standing around a single computer telling the eighth what to do. On the upside, you will have a strong emphasis on knowledge sharing and will possibly improve team communication.

> **eXtreme Programming** · *eXtreme Programming* is a project management method on the team level. It consists of a set of techniques to improve software development speed by having the team work on only one task at a time, having developers work in pairs, and releasing individual features instead of waiting for the full product. It requires an advanced continuous integration system.

XP is a powerful method to consider. Even if you prefer Scrum, I would suggest testing XP as a team exercise. Have your team work on one task together until it is finished, and only then move to the next. It might actually be fun for the team to sit around a single computer and combine their knowledge, solving each problem together.

Chapter 7

A Closer Look at the Numbers

Speed Is Not Necessarily the Issue

A common argument in favor of Scrum is that—once established—the process will produce numbers for business to use in calculations and planning. This is true, and this is the goal: a well-run Scrum process can give you excellent feedback about the "health" of your organization as well as the progress of your projects. But, especially with automated tools like Jira in the background, you can lose perspective. Here, I want to explain statistical, mathematical, and process-related connections to give you reasons for many of the ideas implemented in Scrum.

I remember a question from my math classes: if five workers build a house in 30 days, how many days do 10 workers need? From a project management point of view, this question is of course laughable, as the answer would probably be 30 days because of all the phases involved. Maybe the critical path is 30 days, no matter how many people you throw at the project. From an Agile point of view, the question is very different. Here, it is not about managing cost, quality, or time to fulfill a pre-planned project. Instead, it is about the generated business value per time unit.

The workers could start with the garage so that the family moving into the house could park their car. Maybe they could set up a mailbox so the family could move their postal address. Perhaps they could start by planting the grass early so that when the family moves in, the garden already looks pretty and will not need another month to grow.

Let us say we have a separate test and development team of five people each. Both teams follow every piece of advice inherent in Scrum, except for the fact that they are two teams working on the same user stories. When the development team completes a sprint, it delivers the product to the test team for QA. Let us further suppose developing and testing both take the same amount of time on average and that one sprint takes one week. Upper management then assumes that they have a product ready every two weeks. Compared to what they had before, namely no numbers or release cycle, this system is celebrated as a success. Everyone pats each other on the back. At the end of the year, the actual numbers are compared with the prior year's numbers (without any "controlling," as they had numbers only at the end of each year). Then, management will find that the situation has not improved by much. Likewise, nobody wants to lose face, and they just continue as it is and find rationalizations. It might be said that it was a bad year, it is difficult to find talented people, the lead programmer has quit (but why?), people got sick a lot (but why?), etc., and management leaves things as they are. New Scrum Master hirees are told that the company uses its own version of Scrum and that their proposals to change the process would rock the boat too much.

"Agile."

What happened?

Imagine you have an empty bottle and a full bottle. How do you fill the empty bottle with the water from the full bottle without making a mess? Of course, you use a funnel! But what is a funnel actually? It is a buffer with a limited capacity that ensures a steady flow of water into the other bottle. Having phases with specialized teams is just that: trying to pour water from one into the other, making a huge mess. And there is no funnel to fix that, except to pour so slowly and steadily that no air bubble can form.

What is the "air bubble" in the case of project management? When the first team works faster than the second, work piles up at the second team. When the second team works faster than the first, the second will be idle.

What to do about it? Do you smooth things out by having individual features drop from one team to the next? That helps, but slows things down, and work could still pile up. Do you send your testers to the developers to help out or have developers start testing? You cannot do that, can you? Imagine your top software architect using her time for testing the UI. Or imagine an inexperienced tester taking four times as long as your average programmer to fix a bug in the code. Is there no way but to make a big mess?

What is missing in this evaluation is the business value of things—that is, the value, over time using the product, that the consumer gets. That is a much better indicator of evaluating someone's work than individual speed or efficiency. It does not matter if one part of the whole business works four times faster than the rest; the only thing that matters is how early the final product (or feature) can be used by the customer. So, instead of focusing on local optimization, look at the global picture. No business value is created as long as no customer can use your feature. The goal should be to get one feature through your complete pipeline as quickly as possible, even if that means that some of your resources are under-utilized and not working at 100 percent efficiency.

Scrum solves this by building multidisciplinary teams. But even when you merge two teams (or create two feature teams), you usually end up with each person working on one story, doing everything including programming, writing tests, releasing, etc. While you certainly have solved the problem of idleness of teams—one person is 100 percent involved in the whole chain of production—each story still takes a long time to be developed. In addition, there is little communication between the team members; knowledge management, additional testing (simply by having other people looking at the work), and additional ideas are excluded.

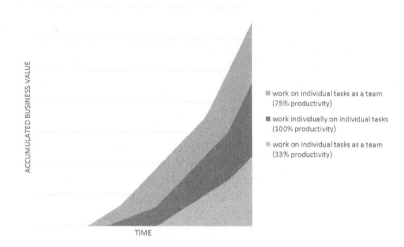

Figure 7.1: Comparison of the accumulated business value of different strategies letting the team members work individually on individual tasks vs. focusing the whole team on individual tasks.

So, are we back at square one with Agile? Let us first draw an example situation into a graph. The challenge is bringing high-value tasks quickly to market (but is that really the challenge in *your* company... another question to ask yourself!). Figure 7.1 shows the accumulated business value of three features if worked on independently by three people, and the accumulated business value of the three features if implemented one after the other by the whole team (first with 75 percent productivity, then with 33 percent productivity). As you can see, if the productivity is still high enough despite the necessary overhead, focusing on finishing individual tasks as a team as fast as possible ultimately shows higher business value returns *on top of* advantages like team building and knowledge sharing!

To summarize, throw the whole team on a task, even if their "productivity" (completed tasks per day) suffers. If it speeds up the delivery of that single crucial feature, you might ultimately end up with higher productivity. Obviously, some calculations are required. But it is important to unlearn the idea of putting individual people on individual tasks simply because they are the ones who can implement them most quickly individually. And we have not even taken into account the internal value of knowledge sharing, more testing, and ultimately higher quality!

Speaking of throwing people on a task: if your team is involved enough in business (a multidisciplinary team involved from design to sales), the team will understand the value of a multidisciplinary team. If it does not, you have another indication that the team is disconnected from the product as a whole, doing local optimizations on their own work without having the larger picture in mind.

How does your team share work among themselves? Do you have specialists, like a "super-programmer"? What is their approach to work optimization?

Chapter 8

Sprinting to Delivery

That Is Waterfall, Not Scrum

> Deliver working software frequently, from a couple of weeks to a couple of months, with a preference to the shorter timescale. Working software is the primary measure of progress. Continuous attention to technical excellence and good design enhances agility.

—Principles Behind the Agile Manifesto[1]

When it comes to Scrum, a central concept is deployment. As a consultant, looking at the deployment process gives me helpful insight into a company's grasp of Agile and Scrum. Depending on the depth of understanding of Scrum and the maturity of the team, the deployment process falls into one of four categories:

- The deployment happens when there is time and when testing is complete, and all the features are merged. A point in time is chosen when the whole project becomes stable or when the team is forced to release for business reasons.
- Deployment happens after a separate testing phase after each sprint, maybe even with a separate release manager.
- Most of the time, the team is ready with testing at the end of the sprint. If it is not, overtime is invested.
- Features can be completed without being stalled by requests from other teams or management.

Ultimately, the question is a philosophical one. What is a sprint? Is it an actual software package delivered to the next department? Is it for business to review? Or is the end of the sprint just a status report to stakeholders?

---

[1]Beck, 2001.

Let us examine:

If the result of a sprint requires an additional confirmation by upper management, why not have them included in the sprint? If the feedback to features comes only at the end of a sprint, valuable time is lost. Additional phases like approval from people outside of the team go against the principles of Scrum. It is the job of the product owner to act on behalf of the stakeholders.

Likewise, it is *not* the job of the product owner to test each story in order to determine if all the *acceptance criteria* have been met. The very idea of coming up with *acceptance criteria* is that the team itself can make decisions about whether or not they met the required function or quality, requiring less interaction with the product owner over time. Finished stories can be demoed to the product owner throughout the day, getting valuable feedback immediately instead of waiting for the end of the sprint. Even a half-finished story can be shown to the product owner if it is clear that the remaining work will not need more input (like documentation, testing additional special cases, etc.).

Approval is one of the jobs of the product owner. And in order to improve the likelihood of achieving approval, *acceptance criteria* and the *definition of done* are formulated. But the workflow should never include assigning testing tasks to the product owner. If you do that, not only does the product owner become the bottleneck, but also you transfer the responsibility for the finished story to him or her. You would train the developer to think that if there were any open issues left, it would be up to the product owner to find them, which moves responsibilities away from the team.

To summarize:

- Neither management nor the product owner should be a phase in development.
- The product owner should review current work during the sprint and give valuable feedback.

Now, back to deployment. Is the goal of the sprint to produce a software package? No! If it indeed produced something at the end, you would actually be employing Waterfall. You would have to do a separate architecture meeting at the end of each sprint to combine all the stories and take care that there are no conflicts, and then do another round of testing to make sure that each feature did not affect another.

Delivery and sprints are independent of each other. The purpose of a sprint is merely to better organize planning. You could hold planning and review meetings for every single story separately, but that would result in significant overhead. Delivery or deployment can be done for each individual story, given you invest enough effort into your continuous integration system. Educate your team in proper branching techniques, organize the code into separate modules, and create stories that do not overlap.

Good luck!

Chapter 9

When Growing Gets Tough

Handling Multiple Teams in Scrum

Applying the principles of Scrum in a larger organization with multiple teams can be challenging. First, it is simply bigger, and having more people involved makes things more complicated. Second, while there is literature on the subject,[1] you can hardly call it a mature system. Third, software support is lacking. So, how do we approach it, using Jira as our preferred tool?

The central element of Scrum is the customer's need—the customer being someone who wants to buy a product from you. The first step is to actually identify what parts of your project are shippable products. If you identify that you have several distinct products, you do not need large-scale Scrum, you can have the teams work independently on the products. Given the easier management, you might even think of splitting existing larger products into smaller ones, but that is a decision requiring knowledge of the architectural details of your project.

Another important element of Scrum is learning. If you have set up multiple teams, they still operate within the same framework, namely the same organization, the same building, or maybe even the same room. Each Scrum Master is running an improvement project that gathers requests by the team and removes impediments (ideally proactively), but at least in my experience, they are hardly ever sharing, except maybe informally through meetings.

One solution to making knowledge sharing possible is to set up one global Scrum Master Jira board that lists the impediments of all teams and have the Scrum Masters work on these tasks as a team. Depending on the volume, you may even require an assistant to help keep that board clean and up to date. This will help the Scrum Masters to encourage each other and reduce duplicated work. Just do not make the mistake of actually physically removing the Scrum Masters from the teams and putting them in their own room: they

[1]Like Larmann and Vodde, 2016.

need to be there for their respective teams, ready to solve any issues.
But while they are waiting for problems to arise, they could help out
the other Scrum Masters clean up the global backlog, or they could
work on impediments found by other teams.

Now, one big issue is specialists or very experienced people in general. They are a rare resource. Previously, we found that it might be
a good idea to keep them on a team instead of moving them into a
management position. With multiple teams, the pressure from the
business side to share specialists among the teams is substantial, as it
is expected that other teams will need to access a particular resource
as well. What to do?

Of course, it depends on the business environment, but if possible,
form a "**support team**" ready to answer questions from any of your
teams—including questions about architecture, legal issues, or technology. This support team works much like traditional customer
support. It builds up a knowledge base and answers questions, ideally as quickly as possible (using management techniques other than
Scrum). This will be the central "brain" of the company for really
tough questions. Depending on the product and the way your company works, you could even merge the support team with your traditional customer support, as they are building up the same kind
of knowledge base, although with the emphasis on the customer.
Last but not least, provide them with the authority to quickly hire
external freelancers in order to have access to specialist knowledge.

With multiple teams and (if applicable) the support team, you might
want to reorganize your **communication** as well. Which tools you
use for that depends on your organization and needs. The question
is who is accessing the support or Scrum team. Ideally, for the initial
request, you will want no direct communication between individual
team members and the rest of the organization. Instead, gather the
requests at a central place and have a manager or the product owner
sort through the issues. I jokingly call this "removing the red tele-

phones" from the desks of the developers.

The most flexible solution is to use a separate email address for questions and problems. This address then can be used by everyone in the company, even those usually not familiar with Jira. This ensures requests will be channeled and minimizes initial training. Then, have either your product owners or Scrum Masters manage those email accounts manually, or use Jira's automatic task creation system. You could promote this email address within the company by arguing that this way, nobody has to figure out who to contact on the team and that there is always somebody who answers questions expediently.

While there is a relatively new functionality in Jira to handle support tickets (service desk), I suggest giving the existing functionality a try. For the internal Scrum and support team communication, you already have many users registered in Jira, so little to no extra configuration is required:

- Set up a POP3 email address (e.g., Gmail)
- In Jira, go to Settings / System / Incoming Mail
- Add POP / IMAP mail server
- For Gmail: Protocol: SECURE_POP, Host name: pop.gmail.com, POP / IMAP port: 995
- Add incoming mail handler
- Handler: Create a new issue or add a comment
- Strip Quotes, Catch Email Address, Bulk: Ignore the email and do nothing, Create Users, CC Watchers

With this configuration, people can use your email address, are automatically added to your Jira user base (to receive comments and make comments themselves via email), and a task is created in the specified project. If you have set up a default assignee in your project (e.g., the product owner), that person gets notified and can then decide whether or not to move the issue to the backlog or to escalate it as a critical bug.

Besides communication, you might want to think about **project organization**. I strongly suggest keeping the organization logical and assigning a Jira project to an actual shippable product. With shippable, I mean *really* shippable. For example, if you have a mobile app and a connected server system, you cannot ship the mobile app on its own. Likewise, installing only the server system without an app might yield zero business value even though it is physically shippable.

Think outside the box, split the "server team" and "app team" into two feature teams consisting of both "server people" and "app people," holding on to the idea of creating multidisciplinary teams. Then, split the project into two features. This could be communication and design, with both teams regularly exchanging codebases or, ideally, working on the same code base and same product backlog on high-priority features. Much more could be discussed in this regard; my point is to really focus on keeping your teams Agile and not fall back into the old Waterfall thinking of compartmentalized component-focused teams working in product phases.

Chapter 10

Daily Scrum with Jira

The daily operation of Scrum is where the more personal qualities of a Scrum Master shine: Humans, not machines, working together to create a product. Here, I want to discuss several small unrelated issues that can easily be fixed. Each of them has only a minuscule effect, yet if you work on them one by one over the course of several weeks, you might improve efficiency by a few percent. *Small steps!*

First, when using Jira—or any other computerized tool—encourage people to use a profile photo and, ideally, their real face. In an organization, people come and go all the time. It saves a few minutes to quickly identify who the person behind the ticket or email is. It encourages people to approach a person in real life. Not everyone is outgoing; some people are shy and might prefer not to discuss something (or to use email instead of direct face-to-face contact) rather than investing energy in finding out who that person is in reality.

Second, attitude. There are two kinds of people: in "socionics" (a personality type theory), there are "democrats" and "aristocrats." The latter type prefers to be asked, the former prefers to ask. No matter who you are as a Scrum Master, you have to be on the asking side. Do not say, "If you have a problem, just come to me." Instead, try to find out about problems proactively. If this is not your area of specialty, perhaps someone from the team has a knack for picking up what problems are currently going on. Talk to him or her!

SOCIONICS · *Socionics* is an advanced personality theory that examines and explains relationships between people. It can be used to describe communication problems and conflicts of interest within a project.

Third: A job well done? Some companies try to bribe team members to perform according to specific goals. But I think money is the last and probably most ineffective way to motivate people. What people want is recognition. Give small (!) bonuses for excellent performance! Sometimes, a meal, snacks, or simply an honestly meant "Good work!" is much more effective than a monetary bribe.

Fourth, a point from stakeholder management: Allow everyone's opinion to be heard. Even if they disagree, they will more likely cooperate if they were given a chance to provide some input. For some decisions, this can be crucial. Maybe refrain from being *too* proactive, and instead learn to listen. Someone whose voice is not heard might find ways to be heard by causing problems or acting as an obstacle, consciously or unconsciously.

Fifth, some (or all) of your team members might work remotely. This can make especially the daily Scrum meetings take longer than necessary. Have them prepare their update in advance in written form for everyone to see. Also, if remote work is a frequent or even permanent situation, consciously use the first five minutes of the daily Scrum for smalltalk. Have the team exchange what they are doing privately, just like they would if they were on site. This is a crucial component for open communication and team building.

Sixth, for longer meetings, use breaks. If you, as a Scrum Master, are an active part of the discussion, it is recommended to use a clock to remind yourself to take a break. One proven method is the Pomodoro technique, which advocates 25 minutes of meeting time followed by five-minute breaks. Get a "buy in" from the team to not use their smartphones during those 25 minutes. Some go even as far as collecting them before the meeting and handing them out during the breaks. That sounds silly, but we all know how dependent we are on them.

> **POMODORO TECHNIQUE** · The *Pomodoro Technique* is a simple time management technique that encourages focusing on one task, followed by a break, then moving on to the next task (Cirillo, 2017).

Seventh, in the daily Scrum, try to NOT use Jira. If your Scrum board is clean, use stickers, even if this is information-doubling. Nobody notices when you move a story in Jira, so have people physically move tasks from one column to the next to demonstrate what they did. And do not forget to discuss the progress of working off the impediment log! It might not be on the board, but these are details that will motivate people as they see that the process is improving.

Your Backlog

Summary and Advice

All books tell a story and this one is no different. Looking back, we started with the origins of Scrum: rugby. Unlike football or soccer, in rugby, there is a strong team emphasis with few to no roles. This is what makes Scrum different from Waterfall. As they say, "It is not the players that make a team win, it is the team that makes the players win." Hiring only specialists and then shifting work from one department to the next is tiresome, especially in today's knowledge-focused industries.

After the introduction, the idea of the "Our Scrum Is Special" chapter was to take away the illusion that you could throw away all the basic project management approaches and invent your own Scrum. The path to implementing Scrum in your company is unique, yes, but your company most probably will face the same challenges as any other. Ultimately, you need to track what parts of Scrum you have implemented. Replace "we do Scrum" with "we are on the path of implementing Scrum."

Having multidisciplinary teams is one big step toward the goal of being an Agile company. Sharing knowledge by working together as a team, removing production phases, and focusing on quick delivery can be achieved by transforming your departments into individual teams that can do everything related to their part of a feature or product.

This leads us to the tools: While the usual approach of using but a pen and paper is replaced by software tools, people tend to forget what Scrum is about. Purposefully not using certain features Jira provides and using specific standards to create new stories will help to remedy that situation. There is a great deal that Jira does (and does not) do, compared to the pen and paper approach and that needs to be addressed. Two examples are the *acceptance criteria* and the *definition of done*. Here, there is often no clear decision made about how to integrate this into Jira for the whole project. So, *definition of done* items exist somewhere in the documentation, or implicitly in people's heads. But with a plugin and some workflow programming, we can automate the *definition of done* in an elegant way. All the information needed to complete a story in one place, great!

With the tools and numbers in order, the focus moves to the team. Often, it is the last (or middle) chain of production—Waterfall. The team is trusted only to play a part in the process instead of being empowered to deliver features on its own. Important decisions are made in management because the best people were moved out of the team and into management roles. With Scrum, it is once again essential to have the team *own* the product. If this is not done, you will face a number of issues.

One particular issue related to ownership is the sprint, its estimation, and the commitment to it. Not without reason was Scrum changed a few years ago to replace "commitment" with "forecast." Striking the right balance between the product owner and the team is crucial. If the team does not own the sprint in its totality, including deciding on its own how to complete it, the team will consciously or subconsciously blame the people who meddled with it. Leading the team making smarter estimations is an excellent way to win over both sides and increase productivity.

All that said, and all work done, it is time for delivery, right? Too often, I see that people confuse Scrum sprints as development sprints. Scrum is the business side, to check on you, to communicate with the client, to plan in chunks, etc. But delivery? That can be done at any time. If you ever encounter a team that delivers at the end of the sprint, you will see several Waterfall elements going on. Keep your eyes open and identify those issues!

As the projects grow, you will also need to add more people and teams to your project. Organizing them in Jira can be tricky, but there are many ways the software can help you to accomplish the task. The most important point is the general organization of your teams.

Finally, there are smart ways to go through your daily Scrum Master routine to help you to do your work better. From psychology to small productivity tips: big things are achieved in small steps.

As the last words, I want to emphasize: refinement. While this is certainly a personal preference, I think a Scrum Master should have the personality of someone who likes to keep things clean and tidy. Small things pile up. Be it trash on the desks or stories that do not belong in the backlog. Walk that extra mile to pick them up—or find someone who volunteers—and your team will love you. It's like running a hotel, you want your guests to feel comfortable and welcome.

That is all for now for *Scrum Your Jira!*, and I hope you can take applicable ideas to your next sprint retrospective meeting to discuss with the team!

Other Books (available in paperback and e-book!)

KANBAN
REMASTERED
Agile Lessons from Strategy Games

8 essays on comparing
Kanban with StarCraft

CLEMENS LODE

How This E-book
Was Created

How I Used Agile to Create a Better Book

This book, like any project, relied on lessons learned from previous projects and yielded lessons for the future. Agile techniques can be applied to a variety of products or services. As pointed out in this book again and again, thinking that such techniques are just for "software people" misses the point of the Agile mindset entirely.

The preceding project to this book was the *Philosophy for Heroes* book series, with the first book *Philosophy for Heroes: Knowledge*. I have to admit that the series initially was planned and executed with everything but Agile methodology, not even proper project management. It was an outgrowth of a hobby which turned into a book. Now that the first part is published, I have had the chance to examine the errata I received from readers and wonder, "How did that happen!?" One curious example is the following:

Was it Bilbo who sailed to the west? Reading *Philosophy for Heroes: Knowledge*, this seems to be the case. On page 5:

Did you know?

In the book series *Lord of the Rings* by J. R. R. Tolkien, the hero Bilbo undergoes a long journey to destroy evil once and for all. Through magical explanations, it is assumed that evil will not return once a magic ring is destroyed. In the story, after the heroic deed is done, the "resolution" for the hero is to sail away to another country and spend the rest of his life there. This idea of a final resolution of a problem is the traditional way of portraying a hero. But in reality, the real task would be only beginning: One would have to ask, how did the people turn evil in the first place? How can we educate them to prevent a similar disaster in the future?

$\longrightarrow$ Read more in *Philosophy for Heroes: Epos*

Now, while the case could be made that Bilbo underwent a heroic transformation, that he fought evil, that he traveled to the west and might have used a boat at some point, the story sounds much more like Frodo's story in *Lord of the Rings*. Myself, I am well versed in fantasy literature, and the amount of media related to the subject is anything but sparse. How could such an error happen?

My usual judgment on products (in this case, a book) is that they are a mirror of the company behind them. If you have a little bit of background information, reviewing a product can be like an archaeological dig. *Philosophy for Heroes: Knowledge* is a multi-layered book. First, it is part of a series. When writing the first book, the other three books had to be kept in mind. In addition, especially being the first book, it had to stand on its own despite its dealing with the basics (philosophy and language). You cannot sell a book called *Philosophy for Heroes* and then tell the reader to wait for part 4 to finally read about what heroism means. Second, it contains a variety of components: study questions, ideas summarizing a section, biographies adding a human element to sometimes abstract explanations, and real life examples. Skimming through the book, those components seem to be "added features" that—while adding value to the book—could just as well be removed. This points to an evolution of the book. Looking back, this is actually true, it underwent a number of transformations:

1. A single, very large book
2. A five-part series
3. Then, a four-part series
4. Then, a four-part series with the first book required to stand on its own
5. Finally, a four-part series, the first book standing on its own, and additional components (study questions, ideas, biographies, examples, etc.)

As this evolution played out, the later changes underwent the least amount of review, while certain parts, that were already finished when devising the initial large book, had so many reviews, the time spent on dragging them along seemed like a waste. How does one write a book without having such a large variance of quality between its parts?

For this, we look at software development. A piece of software faces the same problem: it evolves, some parts are "fresh," others have been looked at and tested for years. The solution people came up with is called "Agile" (with one variant being "Scrum").

The best approach to writing something—anything—is to make sure that its pieces stand for themselves. The advantage of this approach is to have those pieces complete and ready, and you can publish each to get feedback and build an audience. Looking back, I should have published each section of the book separately. Sure, someone could piece all the sections together and then have a copy of the book for free. But that takes a lot of effort. Even if it is just half an hour of work, in that time one could have easily bought the book. Also, the final edit of a book surely connects the independent parts to a greater whole.

In any case, if I had followed the Agile approach, it would have been Frodo, not Bilbo, throwing the ring into the fire and traveling to the West.

Lesson learned.

Lessons Applied

With the mistakes of *Philosophy for Heroes* in mind, this book was created as a web series, with one article released per week. This kept each chapter limited in complexity and scope, kept me and my editor focused on the task, kept any perfectionism in check, and most importantly, we got feedback. After all chapters were written and released, we combined them into an e-book, and re-edited them to fit together. We decided that it is OK to release articles to the web as early as possible. Early adopters can read them online for free, and anyone who wanted a polished version could wait for the e-book. Another great advantage we found is that global design issues—like capitalization of certain words, adding a glossary, and generally streamlining the technical terms—could be tackled later. Lastly, it reduced the urgency toward the end. The chapters were already online and "working" in terms of garnering interest. People got curious about the book while we were still writing it. That, I think, is the power of Agile applied. To summarize, we incorporated:

- bi-weekly chats
- early releases for feedback
- keep perfectionism in check
- keep complexity in check
- market while still writing
- focus on global issues later

And, perhaps the most important point, enjoying a feeling of accomplishment.

Good luck with your project!

The Author

Clemens Lode works as an author as well as a coach for software teams throughout Europe. He lives in Düsseldorf (Germany). You can follow him on Facebook (https://fb.me/ClemensLode) or Twitter (https://www.twitter.com/ClemensLode), or just drop him a line (clemens@lode.de).

 What I cannot create, I do not understand.

—Richard Feynman

Glossary

A

Acceptance Criteria • The *acceptance criteria* are a story-specific set of conditions that need to be met for the story to be accepted and checked off by the product owner. A better expression for acceptance criteria is actually "business-facing tests."

B

Backlog • The *backlog* of a project is a list of stories prioritized by the product owner according to the business value of each (estimated by the stakeholders and product owner) and complexity (estimated by the team). Keeping a clean backlog is key to success: it is not an idea graveyard! You can move all those nice-to-have stories to a separate list.

Bug reports • *Bug reports* are added by anyone testing a released version of the product. They refer to either previous incomplete or erroneously implemented stories or to legacy code not developed with Scrum (or errors resulting from using third-party libraries). For the former, we refer back to the original story; for the latter, we might have to write a new story describing the expected behavior that the new bug contradicts.

D

Definition of done • The *definition of done* is a story-independent list of general tasks that apply to all stories to ensure proper quality assurance, documentation, testing, and so on. This list can grow over time.

Definition of ready • The *definition of ready* is an agreement between the team and the stakeholders (represented by the product owner) that new stories have to conform to a certain standard before they are added to a sprint. It is up to the product owner to make sure that the team has sufficient information to know what the individual story is about and when it is accepted (*acceptance criteria, definition of done*). Obviously, the Scrum Master can help to clean up the stories so that they also conform in terms of visual and grammatical formatting.

I

Issue Checklist for Jira • The *Issue Checklist for Jira* add-on allows users to add simple ToDo list items to an issue and watch the progress when items from the list are completed. It is only available on the Atlassian Marketplace for a Jira Cloud installation (*Issue Checklist* 2017)—check *Simple Tasklists* 2017 for a similar plugin for a Jira Server installation.

J

Jira • The on-premise or cloud software *Jira* by Atlassian is one of the leading ticketing systems available. Beyond a mere ToDo list, it provides administration functionality for projects, Scrum and Kanban boards, custom workflows, custom screens, user rights management, plugins, and third-party integration. The name itself stems from Bugzilla, the software Atlassian used initially for bug tracking. They began calling it by the Japanese name for Godzilla, "Gojira." When they later developed their own bug tracker, they just dropped the Go—hence Jira! (see https://confluence.atlassian.com/pages/viewpage.action?pageId=223219957)

P

PMBOK® • *PMBOK* stands for *Project Management Body of Knowledge* and describes a generic system of workflows within a project. While it is mainly applied to Waterfall projects, many of its parts can also be used in an Agile project, like defining how the team communicates with the outside world, defining the vision and scope of the project, or defining why one would want to use Scrum at all. (PMI, 2013)

Pomodoro Technique • The *Pomodoro Technique* is a simple time management technique that encourages focusing on one task, followed by a break, then moving on to the next task (Cirillo, 2017).

Product owner • The *product owner* is part of the Scrum team and represents the stakeholders. The main task is stakeholder management as well as having a deep understanding of what the project is about and being able to make decisions. A product owner fills and prioritizes the backlog, keeping the complexity estimations of the team in mind. The product owner should have full authority and the final say about the prioritization of the backlog. During the sprint, the product owner answers questions from the team about the scope of the project, as well as gives feedback about finished (but not necessarily done!) tasks, but otherwise does not interfere in how the team manages its work.

S

Scrum • *Scrum* is a set of management tools that focuses a project back on the team level and uncovers internal and external impediments of the production process. By reducing communication paths through small, multidisciplinary teams, as well as frequent releases to the customer for review, the probability for project success can be improved even if the scope is not clear from the start. In addition, work is divided into units of fixed lengths (sprints), which helps to plan future sprints with your team working at a sustainable speed.

Scrum Master • The *Scrum Master* controls the Scrum process. Besides proactively identifying and removing impediments to the process, the Scrum Master also supports the team in meetings as a moderator and individually in personal talks. The Scrum Master also stands up against outside influence on the process, ideally by propagating the Agile idea throughout the organizations and by explaining why certain restrictions are necessary for the overall project success.

Socionics • *Socionics* is an advanced personality theory that examines and explains relationships between people. It can be used to describe communication problems and conflicts of interest within a project.

Sprint • A *sprint* is a timespan of one to four weeks within which a selection of stories should be finished by the team. Given the fact that the whole team spends 10 percent of the time (depending on the sprint length) planning and reviewing each sprint, the goal is to reach 100 percent completion of all stories while meeting the project's quality standards and without overtime. Like a marathon runner needs to carefully plan her energy, planning a sprint requires excellent estimation skills by the teams.

Subtasks • *Subtasks* are specific and usually unique pieces of work related to a particular new feature. If we find that, over the course of many stories, certain types of subtasks repeat, we can elevate them to *definition of done*—like "updated documentation" or "added unit tests."

W

Waterfall • *Waterfall* is a project management method where a product moves through several phases before a final version is finished for release. Compared to Agile, the problem with this method is that it requires additional communication channels between phases. Also, the time until a team or company gets feedback from a customer is generally much longer.

X

eXtreme Programming • *eXtreme Programming* is a project management method on the team level. It consists of a set of techniques to improve software development speed by having the team work on only one task at a time, having developers work in pairs, and releasing individual features instead of waiting for the full product. It requires an advanced continuous integration system.

Bibliography

AgileMethodology (2008). *The Agile Movement*. [online; last accessed Apr 12, 2017]. URL: http://www.agilemethodology.org.

Beck, Kent (2001). *Principles Behind the Agile Manifesto*. [online; last accessed Apr 12, 2017]. URL: http://agilemanifesto.org/principles.html.

Cirillo, Francesco (2017). *The Pomodoro Technique: The Acclaimed Time Management System That Has Transformed How We Work*. Crown Business. ISBN: 978-1524760700. URL: http://amzn.to/2qjDLHM.

Duhigg, Charles (2016). *What Google Learned from its Quest to Build the Perfect Team*. [online; last accessed Apr 12, 2017]. URL: https://www.nytimes.com/2016/02/28/magazine/what-google-learned-from-its-quest-to-build-the-perfect-team.html.

Issue Checklist (2017). [online; last accessed Apr 30, 2017]. URL: https://marketplace.atlassian.com/plugins/com.gebsun.plugins.jira.issuechecklist.

Larmann, Craig and Bas Vodde (2016). *Large-Scale Scrum: More with LeSS*. Addison-Wesley Professional. ISBN: 978-0321985712. URL: http://amzn.to/2oyMEge.

Lode, Clemens (2016). *Philosophy for Heroes: Knowledge*. Clemens Lode Verlag e.K. ISBN: 978-39-4558-621-1. URL: http://amzn.to/2jZxsWK.

— (2019). *Philosophy for Heroes: Epos*. Clemens Lode Verlag e.K. ISBN: 978-39-4558-624-2.

Ohno, Taiichi (2006). *Ask why five times about every matter*. [online; last accessed Apr 12, 2017]. URL: http://www.toyota-global.com/company/toyota_traditions/quality/mar_apr_2006.html.

PMI (2013). *A Guide to the Project Management Body of Knowledge - Fifth Edition*. Project Management Institute. ISBN: 978-1935589679. URL: http://amzn.to/2owDPTe.

Rand, Ayn (1974). *Address to the Graduating Class of the United States Military Academy at West Point New York*. [online; last accessed Apr 12, 2017]. URL: http://fare.tunes.org/liberty/library/pwni.html.

Simple Tasklists (2017). [online; last accessed Apr 30, 2017]. URL: https://marketplace.atlassian.com/plugins/com.topshelfsolution.simpletasklists.

TechTarget (2007). *What is Scrum?* [online; last accessed Apr 12, 2017]. URL: http://searchsoftwarequality.techtarget.com/definition/Scrum.

Index

Is what you are looking for not here? Send us a quick message and help us to improve the index: index@lode.de

An Important Final Note

Writers are not performance artists. While there are book signings and public readings, most writers (and readers) follow their passion alone in their writing spaces at home, in a café, in a library, at the beach, or at a mountain retreat.

*What applause is for the musician, **reviews** are for the writer.*

Books create a community among readers; you can share your thoughts among all those who will or have read this book.

Please leave a thoughtful, honest review and help me to create such a community on the platform on which you have acquired this book. What did you like, what can be improved? To whom would you recommend it?

Thank you, also in the name of all the other readers who will be better able to decide whether this book is right for them. A positive review will increase the reach of the book; a negative review will improve the quality of the next book. I welcome both!

" I believe in you. You can do the thing.